Paper Wasps

Written by Logan Everett

Celebration Press

Parsippany, New Jersey

It is spring. The queen wasp has
been sleeping under the ground.
Now it is time for her to wake up.
She is going to start a colony.

2

A colony is a group of paper wasps that lives and works together. The queen will be head of the colony. Before the queen can start the colony, she must build a paper nest.

She peels wood from trees and chews it. She takes it to the place where she will build her paper nest.

The queen drinks a lot of water. She mixes the chewed wood and water to make a paper nest. Then the queen lays eggs in the nest.

Young wasps from the first eggs to
hatch become workers. Some
workers find food. Some workers
make the nest bigger.

6

eggs

worker

While they work, the queen stays
in the nest and lays more eggs.
More young workers will hatch
from most of these eggs.

Young queens will hatch from some of these eggs. These queens are the only paper wasps that go under the ground for winter. In spring they will come out to make paper nests and start colonies of their own.